Difficult People - How to deal with A-holes at Work, at Home, and at Life

Malcolm Rockwood

DEDICATION

To my Father who; despite my very best efforts, has yet to fail to be there for me.

CONTENTS

ACKNOWLEDGMENTS

We must develop and maintain the capacity to forgive. He who is devoid of the power to forgive is devoid of the power to love. There is some good in the worst of us and some evil in the best of us. When we discover this, we are less prone to hate our enemies.

Martin Luther King, Jr.

1 INTRODUCTION

I want to thank you and congratulate you for purchasing the book, "Difficult People- How to Deal with A-holes at work, home, and at life".

This book contains proven steps and strategies on how to deal with the difficult people in our lives, whether they are colleagues, spouse, parents, kids, neighbors, or friend.

Most of us have dealt with difficult people at least once in our lives. In fact, some of us may have been difficult and unreasonable at one point. But it is important to take note that while almost everyone has exhibited bad and unreasonable behavior at one point of their lives, there are people who habitually exhibit bad behavior.

Difficult people are the people in their lives who have one special superpower- the ability to drain our energy and spread negativity everywhere. They can steal your positivity and make you feel bad about yourself. This is the reason why it is very important to deal with them and remove their power over you. Difficult people are, well, difficult. So it is necessary to get help when dealing with them.

This book will help you deal with the most difficult people in your life. This book will help you understand these people, the psychology behind their bad behavior, and how to deal with them without stepping down to their level or showing hostility.

This book will help you end the pain and suffering that you have been experiencing because of these exasperating, demanding, unmanageable, insubordinate, and obstreperous people. This book will give you tips on how to effectively manage and deal with difficult people in your home, social circles, and work.

Thanks again for purchasing this book, I hope you enjoy it!

2 UNDERSTANDING DIFFICULT PEOPLE

At one point in your life, it is most likely that you have exhibited difficult behavior. You might be a little rebellious when you are young or you occasionally get pissed when the waitress got your order wrong. At one point in your life, you might have shouted at a maid or a customer care representative. It is absolutely difficult to be on your best behavior at all times so there might be times when you just lose your cool.

However, there are people who are difficult, almost all of the time. It's like being difficult is in their DNA. These people are bloodsucking, confidence murderers who would stop at nothing just to get what they want. These people are just toxic and they come in different shape and types.

The difficult person in your life might be your kid, mother, spouse, friend, co-worker, a subordinate, boss, or even a house helper. Difficult people come in different forms. They can be complainers, pessimists, demanding, indecisive, bullies, sarcastic, blamers, people-pleasing, unresponsive, know-it-alls, or hostile. Whatever their characteristics are, one thing is for sure – difficult people create different sorts of problems in your life.

Almost everywhere we go, we will always find people who are negative and who will attack you. So it is necessary that you are equipped with enough information, understanding, and skills to be able to deal with these terrible people.

Why are some people difficult?

Popular motivational speaker Steve Covey wrote that one of the habits of highly effective people is that they seek to understand first before they seek being understood.

To be able to effectively deal with a difficult person, it is absolutely necessary to take a moment to put your feet in their shoes. Not literally, of course. It is really important to understand why they are behaving that way because it is the best way to eliminate a problem is to always look at the root of the problem.

Here are the reasons why some people exhibit difficult behavior:

1. They might be frustrated, tired, or sick - Most people who are suffering from certain diseases have a tendency to be cranky and difficult. People who are also emotionally and physically tired are most likely going to have pessimistic thoughts than those who are relaxed.

2. They might have low self- esteem —Most people who have low self esteem are often shy and do not socialize as much as confident people do. But, some people who have low self esteem increases their self esteem by putting others down. This is the reason why some people who have low self esteem terrorize others just to feel good about their selves. Holding off a task, intimidating, and bullying others make them feel superior. Studies also show that people with low self- esteem are often needy, defensive, anxious, and overly watchful of other people's behavior. People with low self esteem are also passive-aggressive.

3. They might be under the influence of illegal drugs, prescription drugs, or alcohol – People who have been addicted to prescription drugs, illegal drugs, or alcohol often have negative behavioral changes. They are often angry and they get easily irritated. They are also often agitated and hard headed. If you suspect that your loved one or coworker is being difficult or unreasonable because of alcohol or drug addiction, then it is absolutely necessary to make sure that he gets help.

4. They may be going through a difficult phase in their lives - If you ever watch reality shows, you will be able to watch one simple truth play out on TV- people who have problems tend to display rowdy

and difficult behavior. The difficult people in your life might be going through a very difficult phase or situation. Maybe they are going through a divorce, or recovering from the death of a loved one, or suffering from serious financial problems. It is important to understand this so you would be able to deal with these difficult people more effectively.

5.   They may have a mental disorder– People who are suffering from mental diseases and personality disorders such as bipolar disorder, anxiety disorders, obsessive compulsive disorder, paranoid personality disorder, borderline personality disorder, narcissistic personality disorder, anti-social personality disorders, or PTSD tend to be more sensitive, aggressive, and generally more difficult.

Characteristics of Difficult People

If you try to check what "difficult" means in the dictionary, you will get a lot of definitions. It means "needing a lot of effort to deal with", "causing hardships or problems", or "not easy to please". Well, this sounds like someone you know, right? Well, as mentioned earlier, everybody has been difficult at one point of their lives. However, some people in your life may fit these definitions almost all the time. If this is the case, then it is safe to say that they are "difficult people".

Difficult people have different characteristics. In fact, they have different styles and different levels of difficulty. Here are the most common characteristics of difficult people. A difficult person may have only one of these characteristics or more. There are several types of difficult people, which we will discuss later on.

But for now, here are the major categories of A-holes and people who are just plain difficult:

1.   Control freaks – Controllers or control-freaks are people who have a knack of dictating how everything should be done. Most of these control-freaks are perfectionists. They want everything to work their way all the time.

Identifying a control freak is really easy – they will not tolerate resistance of any kind. If someone tries to oppose them, they will do everything in their power to exert and show their dominance. Control freak share different tactics and strategies to get people to do what they want them to do:

- They may play the know-it-all card. They will make it known that they are smarter than everyone else. They would try to intimidate others by projecting that they are more intelligent, more talented, and generally more capable. They may try to use highfalutin words to show that they are superior and will exert and brag about their experience in various fields.

- They may lie. They may omit facts or exaggerate the truth. Anyway, we all know that half-truths are lies. Control freaks lie and deceive others to maintain control. They often go behind other people's back. They backstab people who disagree with them or spread false rumors against them. Some control freaks even cheat just to control and manipulate the outcome.

- They might be aggressive and hostile. They can become too angry and violent. They use their aggressiveness, anger, and violence to retain control. People who want to be at peace would just generally agree with them to avoid conflict.

- They can be passive aggressive – People who are passive aggressive may be appear agreeable and cooperative on the surface. But, they are actually controlling the situation by doing things their way. Passive-aggressive people disobey their superiors by feigning illness, incompetence, or just ignore orders altogether.

2. Self-absorbed people – These people are so preoccupied with their own lives, desires, needs, and dreams that they tend to ignore other's needs and desires. Well, you might say, is it wrong to look after yourself and prioritize your needs and desires? Well, no. In fact, it is our responsibility to look after our own well-being. It is just right that we think about our needs, desires, and ways that we can prosper and make the most out of our lives. In fact, that is really normal and natural as long as your needs and desires are not the only things that you think about.

People who are self-centered are very difficult to deal with. Here are some of the characteristics of self-absorbed people:

- They only focus on their own needs and wants to the point that they don't think about other people's needs. They are totally oblivious of other people's well-being and needs.

- Self-absorbed people are greedy. They want everything to be all about them. They want to acquire whatever they can to fill their needs and wants. They don't care about other people

- They are emotionally needy. They want others to also think about their problems, their wants, their dreams, their needs. They expect other people to be also obsessed with them.

It is generally easy to spot a self-absorbed person because he totally ignores your problems, concerns, and needs. A self-absorbed person will make any conversation all about him.

3. The Stumbling Block Creator – These people are basically obstructionists. They will do everything in their power so that a plan will not work. They often stand in the way and prevent progress. The Stumbling block creators come in different types and have different tactics. Here are some of the tactics that they employ just to create stumbling blocks:

- Stumbling block creators often nitpick someone else's work, the process, or just about anything. They micromanage everyone and examine every detail excessively.

- They move slowly or procrastinate just to delay everything and they do not do their part.

- Some stumbling block creators can be indecisive. Their indecision can delay the creation and production of output. This clogs the whole process.

- They can be eternally negative or pessimistic. They will always give reasons why a certain idea or initiative will not work. They will always look at the possibility that a project or initiative will not work.

4. Ultra-Toxic People – Well, most difficult people are actually ultra-toxic. Their behavior goes far beyond irritating. They are hurtful, emotionally draining, cruel, dismissive, and even ruthless. A toxic person causes pain, turmoil, and confusion in the lives of people around him.

The Ultra-toxic people have many terrible characteristics. Here are some of them:

- They do not keep their word.

- They play games and try to manipulate you.

- These people tell you how to think, feel, and how to do things.

- They use flattery or money to manipulate people.

- At one point, they shower you with flattery and then discard you the moment they get what they want or what they are after.

- They blame the world and other people for their difficulties and problems.

- They refuse to recognize and acknowledge their mistakes.

- They have this grandiose air. They often brag about their skills, looks, and accomplishments.

- They lack character.

- They are imposters. They try to project and be someone that they are not just to acquire your trust and sympathy.

- They exploit your weakness. These people try to take whatever they can for their own gain. They will take advantage of you until nothing's left.

- They lie consistently and shape the reality to serve their own interests.

- They lacked empathy. Although most times, they will just try to feign empathy to get what they want.

- They frequently find fault with people who disagree with them.

- Toxic people will try their best to manage impressions. They will spread false rumors or launch a smear campaign against people that they cannot manipulate.

People who are toxic will make us feel more than irritated. They will make us feel emotionally dumbfounded and numb. They will also make us doubt ourselves and our values. They will make us feel completely worthless, unworthy of love and success. They make us doubt our own intelligence, capabilities, and skills. They will make us feel like we are geared towards failure. They can even make us feel depressed.

Toxic people are very dangerous because they will try to steal something that is very important –your self-esteem. If you happen to be in a relationship with a toxic person, you will often engage in self-destructive behavior like binge-eating, reckless shopping, and drinking too much alcohol.

These are mere categories. We will discuss the different types of toxic people in your life and how to handle specific types.

You have to be equipped with knowledge and skills on how to effectively handle the difficult people in your life. Only then can you reclaim control and be in the driver's seat of your life.

3 KEYS TO EFFECTIVELY HANDLE DIFFICULT PEOPLE

Well, the best advice that one can possibly give in handling difficult people is to just avoid them. This eliminates the problem because you do not have to deal with them and their toxic behavior.

That was ideal. However, life is more complicated. In reality, you cannot avoid the all the difficult people in your life. The difficult person in your life might be your spouse, kid, parent, boss, subordinate, colleague, teammate, or childhood friend. You could not just avoid or abandon your spouse or kid just because they are being difficult. Or quit a job that you really like just because your boss or your subordinate feels that it is cool to impersonate the devil.

Here are some of the general strategies that you can use in handling or dealing with very difficult people. Remember that these are just general principles. We will go into specific types and how to deal with them later on.

1. Focus on yourself, build self-knowledge, and strengthen your emotional intelligence – There's a popular saying that it is almost impossible to upset or push the buttons of a person who knows himself completely. Before you could effectively deal with a very difficult person, it is absolutely necessary to look within yourself first. You have to know what your buttons are –what upsets you, what makes you sad, what makes you jealous. Most difficult people are manipulative and they will keep on pushing your emotional

buttons. When you have mastered yourself and your emotional buttons. When you have mastery over your emotions, it is not easy to manipulate you. Not even yelling, violence, or a nasty smear campaign can make you crumble.

2. Acknowledge that the person is being difficult – Sometimes, you will make excuses for the other person. Before you could effectively handle a difficult person, you must first acknowledge the fact that their behavior is unacceptable and that these people can be dangerous because they can take away your self-esteem and sometimes, even your sanity.

3. Seek to understand them – As mentioned earlier in this book, it is important to understand them and where they are coming from. Are they having a bad day or a bad life? Are they going through a divorce? Walk in their shoes. Difficult people are really hard to deal with. Think Meryll Streep in The Devil Wears Prada. But while they are difficult, they are people, too. They have feelings, too. Once you understand why these people act the way they do, it will be easier to deal with them. You could deal with them in a more peaceful way. No bloodshed needed.

4. Validate them- While this strategy doesn't work and must not be used on some types, validation can be a powerful tool that you can employ to effectively deal with a difficult person. Most people are being difficult because they felt insignificant and they feel that they are not heard or understood. This is the reason why it is important to validate a difficult person's feelings, ideas, and situation. Validation can do wonders. Validating and listening to a difficult person can make him feel important and significant. For most difficult people, this is the best way to move forward. But remember that when you validate, it doesn't mean that you agree with their ideas or behavior. It just means that you are listening and that you understand where they are coming from.

When you are listening to a difficult person, it is important to tilt your head slightly. This is because the person will feel heard and understood when you slightly tilt your head. Also, nod and acknowledge their statements every now and then. This will assure the other person that you are listening and that you understood.

5. Don't resist – Fighting will not work for most difficult people. It will only make matters worse. When you are dealing with a difficult

person, it is important to stay calm and collected and be the bigger person. Think of the consequences before you do anything.

6. Bond with them- If the difficult person in your life is your spouse, kid, or parent, a great way to deal with them is to bond with them. This will allow them to be more open with them and this will allow you to be more open with you. You can arrange a beach outing or hiking. Spending more time with a difficult person will allow you to understand him more.

7. You can use strategic influence- One way to effectively deal with a difficult person is to know who influence them. You must know who they listen to, the people they respect. Once you find out who they actually listen to, you might be able to get some tips on how to effectively handle the difficult person.

8. Downplay – Do not fight fire with fire. Do not respond with long emails and long speeches. Do not call out the person's behavior with a bold and grand gesture or reply. Just listen and respond calmly. Do not feed negative behavior by responding in a grand manner.

9. Exhibit Self Confidence – Difficult people feed on your weakness so it is absolutely necessary to display confidence when dealing with them.

10. Do not take things personally – Sometimes, their behavior is not about you at all. As mentioned earlier, difficult people might be having a rough time.

These keys would help you deal with the most difficult people in your life. When you are dealing with a difficult person, you should not have the fight or flight response. People with difficult behavior should be dealt with head on. But, of course, in doing so, you have to be the bigger person and you should not in any way stoop down to their level.

4 DIFFERENT TYPES OF DIFFICULT PEOPLE AND HOW TO DEAL WITH THEM

We have already discussed the different categories of difficult people. In this chapter, we will discuss the some of the types of difficult people and how to deal with them.

The Howitzer

The Howitzer is confrontational. He is always angry and he can be very pushy. He is often aggressive.

Action Plan

Your goal when dealing with the Howitzer is to command respect. When you are verbally assaulted, insulted, accused, or attacked, your primary response is to command respect. Why? Very simple. The Howitzer does not attack or verbally assault people they respect, admire, and look up to. When you are dealing with a very aggressive person like the Howitzer, it is very important to stay calm but stand your ground. You must send a clear message that you are capable, smart, and strong and that you will not be taking any BS. If you appear weak, you are inviting and encouraging further attacks. If you appear annoyed, irritated, or you exhibit the same aggressive behavior then not only is it a sign of weakness but you may incur a physical confrontation, so it is extremely important to stay calm.

When you are being attacked by the Howitzer, stay put. Listen and look at him in the eyes. Breathe. This is important so that you can maintain self-control. Then, interrupt the attack by repeating the Howitzer's name silently over and over until they stop. Once you have his attention, restate his points. This will assure him that you are listening to what he is saying and then go to the bottom line. You can say something like "I understand you, but in my point of view...". Then, offer a peaceful solution.

Remember, the more that you are calm, the more he will respect you. It is important to be assertive, calm, and you should not be emotional.

His Highness, King Know-it-All

The Know-it-all could not tolerate contradiction or even correction. There are two types of know it all. The first is the Know-it-all who really knows his stuff. The second is one who pretends to know it all to intimidate others.

Action Plan:

When you are dealing with a Know-it-All, your goal is to make him accept to new information and ideas. There will be days when you have better ideas than the Know-it-all so it is absolutely necessary to make him open his mind and make room for new ideas and information.

When you are dealing with the Know-it-all, you have to be prepared. You have to know what you are talking about or else, you will be eaten alive. The Know-it-all has a standard defense mechanism – scrutinize, criticize, and nitpick new information. He will try to discredit your ideas. If he has doubts about your idea, remember to address those doubts head on.

Lastly, one strategy that you can do is to turn King Know-it-all into a mentor. Do this if the King Know-it-all is actually very smart. This will lower down his defenses.

The Complainer

No one really wants to be with a complainer. Complainers always think that the world is unfair and that they are helpless. They always complain about anything and they can be ungrateful, too. They always see the glass as half empty.

Action Plan:

When you are dealing with a complainer, it is necessary to work with them to find a solution to the things that they are complaining about. Remember this, do not agree with complainers. This will just fuel their baseless complaints. Always look for constructive ways to deal with this problem. Take command and control the conversation, but be tactful.

The Yes Man

The Yes Person is actually a people pleaser who can't say no. They over commit, to the point of taking themselves for granted. They tend to take more projects than they could deliver and this will ultimately delay the delivery.

Action Plan:

Your goal when you are dealing with a yes person is to create a safe environment where it is ok to say no when they are really unable to deliver. Also, be honest with him. Let him know that you'd rather prefer that he is honest with you than committing to something that he could not deliver. Ensure commitments and strengthen your relationship with him.

The Indecisive

The Indecisive person holds off any decision because they believe that a better choice will come their way someday. Well, as we all know, some decisions must be made quickly. It might be too late when the Indecisive person finally makes a decision.

Action Plan:

Your goal is to help them become more decisive by clarifying options. Present the pros and cons of every outcome. If the person really has difficulty in making choices, teach him a decision making system. Listing the pros and cons could be a good decision making system.

5 DEALING WITH DIFFICULT PEOPLE AT WORK

After learning about the kinds of difficult people that you encounter in your life in general and how you should deal with them, you should now learn some effective tips on how to deal with these a-holes at work. You often hear about people complaining about their dictator boss or their gossipmonger coworker. Some bosses also complain about useless employees who receive generous salary every month but contribute nothing significant to the growth of the company. It is also important to know how to deal with these specific kinds of difficult people in your office. Your work will be so much easier if you get along with everyone else.

It is not enough that you are good with your work because you also have to be good at dealing with coworkers. Many people who work in a corporate environment believe think that the most stressful part of their job is the people they work with. This may sound too harsh especially when you are getting along really well with your coworkers but many people have at least one a-hole in their office that they have to work with. You can say that these people are difficult when they prevent you from performing your best or when working side by side with them feels like torture.

You have to know the different types of difficult people that you may encounter in your office. It is important to know right now that it is not your responsibility to change them. You can only change your attitude or mindset that will help working with them a lot easier.

The slacker

It is okay to slack off from time to time, like once in a blue moon. However, those people who make a habit of slacking off are the ones you should look out for. These people hate work like the plague. They will try to get as little work as possible done and give the rest of their tasks to their coworkers who do not know how to say no. They lack the initiative to start working on a project and often miss deadlines and submit their work late.

The slacker is bad for the company because productivity is affected. It is also a hassle to work with a slacker because you will always end up doing all the work while he does things that slackers often do, like wasting their time browsing through pictures of cats online or stalking their friends using their social media account. If you belong in the same team, you and the other members will often end up doing all the work because the slacker's finished project is often embarrassingly subpar, which will only pull the whole team down.

What you can do:

You should focus on your work and responsibilities alone. You need to stop enabling the slacker's behavior by letting him do his own responsibilities. You should stop picking up the slack because the slacker will only get used to this and will always think that he always has your back. If you belong in the same team and each of your work will affect the team's productivity, you need to tell your supervisor or your boss about this before you take on extra responsibility. This way, credit will be given to where it is due. And the slacker will be reprimanded and taught a lesson.

The Ultracompetitive

There is nothing wrong with being competitive. In fact, a lot of companies encourage a little healthy competition among their employees and their teams by having contests, giving rewards, and acknowledging excellent performance. It only becomes bad when someone becomes ultracompetitive. The ultracompetitive coworker is someone who will do anything to get that promotion. He will stab you in the back, start some rumors about you, or suck up to your boss to get what he wants. They are selfish and only have their best interest at heart and do not care if they step on someone whom they think is blocking them from their success.

What you can do:

If you are working with this type of person in a team, you should always have your eyes and ears open because he might view you as a rival and you might end up being the subject of his backstabbing ways. You should just ignore what this person is doing and just focus on doing your best. Do not stoop down to his level. You should only ask for his help only when you absolutely have to. You need to accept the fact that he works differently than you. If you are the boss, you can turn this competitiveness to your team's advantage.

The fraud

You need to look out for the fraud in your office because this person loves to brag and exaggerate to make him look more impressive. They will lie about their accomplishments or add or subtract some information here and there to make them look so much better than they actually are. They talk about their accomplishments all the time but they have yet to prove themselves in the office. It is annoying to work with the fraud because it is annoying enough when someone brags about their REAL accomplishments. It is even more annoying if those accomplishments are not real at all. You will also start to wonder what other things this person lied to you about. And it is difficult to work with someone who does not tell the truth or who always tells half truths.

What you can do:
There's really not much you can do but to ignore the fraud in the office. Just go along with his stories but do not believe in everything that he says. However, if his fakeness goes too far, like claiming the project that you worked hard for as his own or if he is trying to get all the credit for a team project where everyone has his own contribution, then it is time for you to step up and defend yourself.

The gossipmonger

You can always find the gossipmonger in almost any workplace. This person loves to talk about other people's life or start rumors that are not true. It could be because they feel bored or they just love the thrill of spreading juicy gossip about the people they work with. It is difficult to work with the gossipmonger because it can create conflict among coworkers because of the false rumors and it can distract employees from doing their job.

What you can do:

You should just ignore the gossipmonger politely if he starts talking to you about a coworker. Just tell him in not so many words that you are not interested. You should also avoid sitting with the gossipmonger during lunch break because it will be like reading a tabloid or watching gossip shows on TV for an hour. If you are the subject of the rumors that this coworker started, you should confront him about it. If you are the boss, you should make it a point to keep the employees busy to avoid gossiping during office hours.

The aggravating boss

Many employees complain about their boss at one time or another. Some may get along well with their boss but still dislike some aspects of their boss' behavior while others simply hate their boss' guts. It is understandable to view the boss as the villain in the office because he is the one assigning the tasks, giving reprimands and memos, and creating rules and policies in the office. However, there are really some bosses who really have a difficult personality which makes it hard to work with them.

What you can do:

You should do your best at all times so that your boss will not have anything against you. Always follow the deadline, submit high quality work, be respectful, and be a team player. Your boss will most likely hold open forums where you can give feedbacks about the way he manages your team. You should take this opportunity to share your thoughts and feelings but be sure that you do it in a respectful and polite way. You do not want to antagonize your boss because he is still your boss and you work for him. You still have to tread carefully if you want to keep your job.

6 DEALING WITH DIFFICULT PEOPL AT HOME

The next thing that you need to learn is how to deal with difficult people at home. It is hard enough when you have to work with crazy people at the office. It is even more difficult if you have to live with the same kind of people in the same house. There are also difficult people that you have to live with at home like your partner, your parents, your siblings, and your kids. It is more difficult to handle situations or conflicts with them because these are the people you love and care about. When a coworker is behaving like an a-hole, you can simply ignore him and not talk to him the whole time you are in the office. You cannot simply do this with your loved ones. You cannot just stop talking to your parents or ignore your kids especially if you live with them. Some people are okay with this but it is a huge emotional burden to carry if you are not in speaking terms with one or some of your family members.

You need to know how you can deal with you loved ones who are difficult to live with. This way, you can avoid conflict and misunderstandings that can do damage to your relationship.

Parents

There are different kinds of parents but most kids complain about their parents who are too strict or controlling. Strict or controlling parents are those who do not allow their kids to go on dates without a chaperone or who only allow their kids to have a boyfriend or girlfriend when they finish college. They are also those who control your life from the food you eat, the clothes you wear, and your major in college. You never really noticed when you were a child but as you grow older, you start to feel choked with all the rules that you need to follow and with your parents always meddling in your life.

What you can do:

First and foremost, you need to remember that your parents love you very much and they are only doing these things out of love. This will prevent you from hating your parents, like many kids with controlling parents do. You need to always be respectful with your parents no matter what because they are your parents. You also need to watch your language when communicating with them. Do not get all too defensive when they ask you a question. If your parents are being unreasonable, you should sit down and talk to them. It will not do you any good if you start yelling, slamming the door, or stomping your feet because it will only give them further reason to control because you are showing immaturity. If you want to gain their trust so that they will stop being controlling, you should show them that you are mature enough to deal with your problems in an adult way. You should also avoid doing things that will make them lose their trust in you.

Siblings

Your brothers and sisters can also be difficult to live with. You love your siblings but there are times when you wish you are an only child! Some have to deal with siblings who are lazy and do not want to do their share of house chores while others have ultracompetitive siblings who competes with you in every little thing you do. There are also those who are jealous of your accomplishments and those who meddle in your personal affairs. These kinds of siblings make your life at home difficult. It is just like living in the office with the crazy people described in the previous chapter but ten times worse because you get to live with them 24/7.

What you can do:

You need to accept the fact that people are wired differently. However, there is a difference between acceptance and tolerance. You should accept the fact that your sister is lazy but you should not tolerate this kind of behavior. For example, you need to accept that she hates housework but you need to work out some kind of system, like assigning her chores that she prefers or giving her some kind of rewards, to ensure that she gets her share of work and that you do not pick up every time she slacks off. If you have a jealous or competitive brother, you should just get it over it especially if it is harmless. You may need to talk to him if you think it is affecting your relationship but try to ignore it as much as you can. You should also avoid one upping your brother all the time that can further provoke his jealous or competitive behavior.

Teenagers

If you are a parent and you are asked to think about difficult people at home, you probably automatically think about your teenage kids. Everyone knows that the teenage years are the most difficult to deal with for parents. This is the time when kids view their parents as the villains in their lives and they would rather be with their friends than with mom or dad. This is also the time when kids get curious (or get pressured by their peers) to try new things like smoking, drinking alcohol, and sometimes, doing drugs. They tend to shut their parents out and prefer to tell their problems to their friends because they think parents are the enemies.

What you can do:

As a parent, it is important that you know how to handle your rebellious teenagers because this will have an impact in their adult life. It is important to make them feel that you are not the enemy by leaving the communication line open and making sure that you listen to them when they speak. Avoid threatening or yelling at them because this will only push them further away. It is important to show that you respect them because this is something that they want from their parents. You should also give them enough privacy by not spying on their every move. Finally, you need to always remind yourself that you are, first and foremost, their parent, and not their friend. You need to give them enough space but you should also impose limits that will teach them later on in life how to follow rules when they are adults.

Young children

Being an adult who is married and has children seems more trouble than it's worth. First, you have to deal with annoying coworkers and boss. Next, you have to deal with rebellious teenage kids. And most parents also have to deal with young children. Just wait because the next topic in this chapter will be about dealing with difficult spouses or partners. You often hear about the phrases 'terrible twos' or that short period when your once sweet and cuddly baby turns into a monster. They start to throw tantrums or act stubborn and disobedient.

What you can do:

In every problem that involves your child, whether they are teenagers or young kids, it is important to show and remind them that you are doing the things that you need to do because you love them. You need to always be patient when dealing with difficult children. Easier said than done especially in situation when you feel like tearing your hair out or jumping off to the nearest bridge but that's how it works. You need to be calm when reprimanding your child. Instead of using corporal punishment, you should use timeout by letting your child sit on a chair or face the wall for a certain period of time. It is also important not to give in to your child's demands. Most of the time, young children throw tantrums because they think they can cry their way to get their needs. If you stand firm and do not give in, your child will realize that throwing tantrums does not work.Finally, it is important to talk to your spouse or your partner when it comes to dealing with your kids. You need to show a united front that will not confuse your children.

Spouse or partner

There are also times when your spouse or partner is the one that gives you headaches at home. You probably go home to a controlling or jealous husband or a nagging or clingy wife. There are also times when people live with a highly critical spouse who does nothing but criticize their every move. If you have a spouse who can be considered as difficult, you need to learn a thing or two on how to deal with this issue. If it's any consolation, there are many people who also have the same problem at home. You need to know what you can do to improve your situation.

What you can do:

In any relationship, communication is extremely important. Instead of complaining about your spouse to your friends or keeping all your issues bottled up inside, you need to consider letting all out and telling your spouse how you feel. Just remember to stay calm and respectful when you talk to each other. Do not be defensive or antagonistic because this will only make the problem worse. It is also important to avoid saying hurtful words that you will regret later. This is why it is never a good idea to talk when you are angry or hurt.

You also need to do your part to make your relationship work. Maybe your spouse has a reason to be jealous because you are not being completely honest. Or maybe you never do the things that you promise you would do that's why your spouse always ends up nagging you. You also need to take a closer look at yourself to see if there are things that you need to change. But after having numerous serious talks, trying to work things out, and even going to a marriage counselor, and still your problem persists, you may need to consider getting a divorce because it is possible that you would be better off living apart than living together. But keep in mind that this should only be your last resort; only after you have exhausted every possible solution to your problems.

7 DEALING WITH DIFFICUL PEOPLE THAT YOU MEET IN YOUR EVERYDAY LIFE

Aside from the people at work at and at home, you will also come across a number of difficult people in your life outside these places. This last chapter will focus on the people that you interact with regularly that can be difficult to deal with. Some useful tips and information are provided that can help you survive being in the same room with them.

Friends

Friends come in different shapes and sizes. There are great friends that you consider your best friends then there are those friends who are not necessarily bad but are difficult to deal with. There are friends who are too self-absorbed thinking that the world revolves around them, friends who are big blabbermouths and keeping a secret is not in their vocabulary, friends who make a lot of promises but break just as many, and friends who view your friendship as a competition. You probably have at least one of these people in your circle of friends. You need to know how to deal with them to ensure that your friendship will not be affected.

What you can do:

Most of the time, the best way to deal with difficult friends is to be honest about your issues with them. For example, you should tell the self-absorbed friend that you also need to share things about your life from time to time and that you should learn how to give and take in your friendship. You need to tell the promise breaker how you feel hurt and disappointed every time he breaks his promise. There are also different ways to handle them. For example, if you know that your friend is an incurable blabbermouth, just try not to tell her your deepest, darkest secrets, such as the dead body in your basement or something just as dark. For the overly competitive friend, you should also avoid bragging too much about your accomplishments that can provoke his ultracompetitive behavior. It is important to have an open communication with your friends if you want to keep the friendship.

However, there are some kinds of difficult friends that are not worth keeping, such as the double-crosser who stabs you in the back so many times or the faultfinder who always seem to find it difficult to say positive things about you.

Teachers

If you are a student, you will also come across at least one difficult teacher in your life. These are teachers who are difficult to please no matter what you do. You can submit your homework on time or write an essay worthy of the Pulitzer Prize but still give you a really low mark. There are also teachers who embarrass students in front of their class. It is even more difficult if the teacher is singling you out from the rest of the class.

What you can do:

You first need to evaluate yourself whether or not you are doing something wrong. Maybe you are being disrespectful or maybe you do not take your teacher's projects seriously. If the teacher gives you a low score on something, you should ask him about it so that you will know how you can improve next time. Remember to always be polite and respectful when talking to your teacher no matter how much of an a-hole he is.

If you think you are the epitome of a perfect student and your teacher cannot provide you with a valid reason for your low grades, and you think the teacher still hates your guts, you might want to consider talking to your guidance counselor about it. Before talking to your guidance counselor, you might bring some proofs like your perfectly written essay graded with a D or anything that can support your case.

Neighbors

Your neighbors are people you don't exactly live with but they are a part of your daily life because they just live next door. Some of them are really nice, like those neighbors who will watch over your house when you are away on vacation or who always lets you borrow sugar or flour. Then there are those difficult neighbors who make you want to relocate to a different state. There are those neighbors who do not care if their dogs poop in your yard or neighbors who always play loud rock music. There are also those neighbors who devalue your neighborhood by not mowing their lawn, not doing any repairs, or leaving that rusty old car to acquire more rust in their front yard.

What you can do:

The first thing to do is to talk to your neighbors about it. Tell them as politely as you can that the loud rock music always wakes the baby up or that their dog always poops on your lawn. If you cannot talk to your neighbor in person because of conflicting schedule, you can leave a polite note on their door. There was this one situation where the neighbors decided to talk to one of their neighbors who does not take care of their lawn and makes the entire block look rundown and unkempt. After talking to the homeowner, they found out that she and her partner were having a divorce and she was undergoing cancer treatment. The neighbors decided to pitch in and help clear her front yard. Sometimes, thing aren't always what they seem so it is best to talk it out first with the people concerned.

8 CONCLUSION

Thank you again for purchasing this book!

I hope this book was able to help you to deal with the difficult people in your life and reclaim control in your life.

The next step is to apply the easy to follow tips and strategies contained in this book. When you follow the strategies contained in this book, you will effectively handle the different types of difficult people in your life.

This is the time to stop the pain and suffering caused by these horrible people. It is time to stand your ground, address the situation, and become the bigger person. When you follow the tips contained in this book, you will be surprised with the sudden changes in your home, work, and social life.

Finally, if you enjoyed this book, please take the time to share your thoughts and post a review on Amazon. It'd be greatly appreciated!

Thank you and good luck!

9 PREVIEW OF: CHEATING SPOUSES - HOW TO DEAL WITH IT AND WHAT TO DO AFTER THE FACT

Chapter One

Understanding the Concept of Marriage

While many couples still dream of entering into a marriage and hopefully live happily thereafter, their aspirations are often shattered by the harsh reality that approximately three-fifths of marriages fail, and one of the major reasons is infidelity. In fact, statistics reveal that nearly 60% of married men and women have been found to commit infidelity. Some marriages may actually recover from it, but others do not. Before infidelity can be dealt with, it is first necessary to understand why it is such a big deal. What makes it so wrong? In order to find the answer, it is important to understand the concept of marriage from which the injury of infidelity is derived.

Marriage is the lawful union of two individuals. It is generally entered into by a man and a woman, although in recent developments some states allow now allow same-sex marriages. There are many reasons why people get married. While convenience, financial stability, property expansion and other protections conferred by the federal government, state laws and employers may be included, love is still the underlying cause for many. In fact, in a survey conducted by Pew Research in 2010, more than 90% of married people in the United States alone still consider love as the major reason for getting married with more than 80% of unmarried Americans affirming the same. Hence, it has a twofold foundation: love and justice.

Marriage as an Act of Love

As a commonly used word, love is simply associated with a strong feeling of fondness toward someone. In relation to marriage, love is described in the Stanford Encyclopedia of Philosophy as the desire to form an important union. However, there are several views of love as a union. One reason for infidelity is because spouses may differ in their views of love. One view is that the distinction between individual interests disappears when the couple begins to have shared concerns, where they act for their unified sake. Another view is that each individual redefines himself according to the relationship by playing significant roles in the new life they share. An alternative view also states that the union created dissolves their individuality where the well-being and autonomy of each is now entwined with that of the other.

Infidelity occurs when couples do not accept the union view. Many people enter into marriage arguing that undermining the individual's autonomy is bad since love requires having respect for the other's autonomy. However, proponents of the "love as union" view counter that the loss of independence is an acceptable effect of love. It is neither selfishness nor self-sacrifice because by eliminating the distinction between individual interests, reciprocity is produced by turning each other's interests into one's own.

Marriage as a Legal Contract

Under the requirement where it must be voluntarily entered into by mutually consenting individuals, marriage likewise entails couples to fulfill the oaths they undertake. It is a legal contract. One of the vows which make cheating unacceptable is the vow of fidelity as it is one of the obligations arising from providing each other with mutual respect. Violating the contract is committing an injustice to the other.

In the end, it will all boil down to what an offended spouse values more: justice or love? As for the offender, he or she clearly values none.

10 CHECK OUT THE OTHER BOOKS BY ME

Below you'll find some of my other popular books that are popular on Amazon via paper back and Kindle as well. These are the titles of them which can be found by going to www.Amazon.com and typing Malcolm Rockwood into the search bar.

Learning New Languages - The easy way to learn it, use it, and love doing it!

Interview Clothes - What to Wear and What Not to Wear to Get your Dream Job

Let's Buy a House! - The In's and Out's to Know for a First Time Home Buyer

Navy Boot Camp Survival Guide - How to Survive the Worst Eight Weeks of Your Life

Pet Ownership - Everything You Need to Know to Become Your Pet's Dearest Human.

Cheating Spouses - How to Deal With it and What to do After the Fact

Difficult People - How to Deal with A-holes at Work, at Home, and at Life

Mobile Apps- How to make them, sell them, and have fun doing it!

House Rules - Survival Guide to Living with Roommates

ABOUT THE AUTHOR

Born in Texas and raised all over the country Malcolm Rockwood never stayed in one place for long. After moving from Texas to New Mexico and then back to Texas he attended high school in Naples Florida. During college he made the leap and joined the United States Navy where he saw the world. After serving six years he left the United States Navy honorably but took a lot from the United States Navy with him to include his wanderlust. He continues to travel the world seeking things he doesn't know but understands he will know when he sees it.

He currently resides in the state of Missouri

Printed in Great Britain
by Amazon.co.uk, Ltd.,
Marston Gate.